To Parents

Bears, dolls, diggers, trains… all the favourite toys
are included in this delightful collection
of playtime words.

Help children to develop reading and language
skills by looking through the book together.
Encourage them to look closely at the pictures,
spot similarities and differences, and.
to talk about what they see.
Children will soon learn to recognise
the images and enjoy matching
the words to the pictures.

A catalogue record for this book is available
from the British Library

Published by Ladybird Books Ltd
A subsidiary of the Penguin Group
A Pearson Company
© LADYBIRD BOOKS LTD MCMXCIII

LADYBIRD and the device of a Ladybird are trademarks of
Ladybird Books Ltd Loughborough Leicestershire UK

First

words
for me

illustrated by GAYNOR BERRY

Ladybird

blocks

planes

balls

trains

teddy bears

cars

dolls

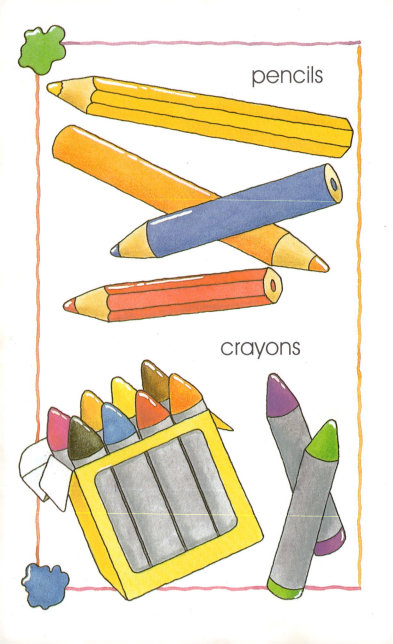

pencils

crayons

paintbrush

red powder paint

paints

hammer

saw

screwdriver

screws

bolt

telephones

tractor

boat

digger

fire engine

jack-in-
the-box

Humpty
Dumpty

trolley

tricycle

books

puzzles

roundabout

see saw

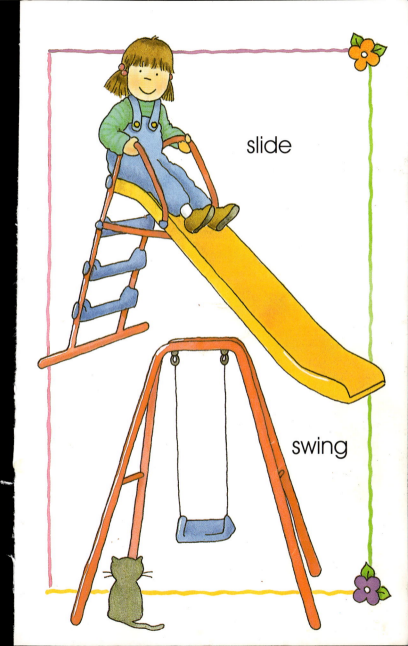

slide

swing

balls
blocks

boat
bolt
books

cars
crayons
digger

dolls
fire engine
hammer
Humpty Dumpty

jack-in-the-box
paintbrush
paints
pencils